World Crafts and Recipes

Recipe and Craft Guide to

ITALY

Julia Harms

Mitchell Lane

Mitchell Lane

World Crafts and Recipes

The Caribbean • China • France
India • Indonesia • Israel
Italy • Japan • South Africa

Copyright © 2012 by Mitchell Lane Publishers

Library of Congress
Cataloging-in-Publication Data applied for

PUBLISHER'S NOTE: The facts on which the story
in this book is based have been thoroughly
researched. Documentation of such research
can be found on page 60. While every possible
effort has been made to ensure accuracy, the
publisher will not assume liability for damages
caused by inaccuracies in the data, and
makes no warranty on the accuracy of the
information contained herein.

To reflect current usage, we have chosen to
use the secular era designations BCE
("before the common era") and CE ("of the
common era") instead of the traditional
designations BC ("before Christ") and AD
(*anno Domini*, "in the year of the Lord").

ISBN: 9781612280837

eBook ISBN: 9781612281698

Printing   1   2   3   4   5   6   7   8   9

PLB

CONTENTS

Introduction

Bella Italia

Bella Italia—land of beauty and style, of pizza and gelato, of ancient Rome and the Italian Renaissance, of la dolce vita and some of the best soccer teams in the world.

Italy today has 60 million inhabitants and is divided into 20 regions, with the capital, Rome, in the western region of Lazio. It is a peninsula shaped like a long boot starting in Europe's Alps in the north, then stretching southeast into the Mediterranean Sea. The country is about the size of Arizona with a coastline that is over 4,700 miles (7,560 kilometers) long. Sicily, the biggest island, lies, fittingly, like a soccer ball at the tip of the boot's toe.

Regional differences, such as in dialects and cuisine, are very strong. In the north, for example, polenta (a dish made of boiled cornmeal) is used a lot, whereas in the south, pasta is the main starchy food. In parts of the south, such as Apulia and Campania (the area around Naples), you will find more spicy food compared to the milder food of the north. On restaurant menus on the coast you may find nothing but fish and seafood but going inland just a few miles you will find amazing meat dishes.

The Vatican—the governing body of the Catholic Church—lies in the center of Rome. Although it functions as its own city-state, run by the Pope, its influence is felt throughout the country. Most Italians are Roman Catholic, which is reflected in their holidays. Twelve days after Christmas, on January 6, they celebrate Epiphany or Three Kings Day, when the Three Wise Men visited the baby Jesus in the manger. Ash Wednesday marks the beginning of Lent, forty days of fasting and penitence that end on Easter. The day before Ash Wednesday is often called Fat Tuesday (*Martedì grasso*), as it is the last day of feasting before the more solemn period of Lent. Fat Tuesday is the culmination of Carnival. Also, every village and town has its own patron saint who is celebrated on his or her special day every year.

ITALY

Where in the World

Italy is a modern democracy much like the United States, but what we now call Italy has gone through many changes in history. In fact, it was not one united country until 1861.

The Italian peninsula has been settled since prehistoric times, of which the ancient stone constructions called Dolmen and Menhir are proof. Between 1700 and 1100 BCE, the first Greeks arrived. By about 800 BCE, more Greeks had colonized parts of southern Italy and Sicily. You can still find Greek-speaking communities in southern Italy, in Apulia and Calabria.

At this time, ancient Rome was a small agricultural community, but it grew into a huge empire. It eventually encompassed the land around the whole Mediterranean Sea, reaching as far as England in the north, North Africa in the south, and modern Iraq in the east. Rome became the hub of western civilization. Italy is the land of Julius Caesar, aqueducts, amphitheaters, and gladiators.

Besides the great works of art from ancient Rome, we also have a clear window into how the Romans lived from the ruined sites of Pompeii, Herculaneum, and Stabiae, which are close to modern-day Naples. Mount Vesuvius erupted in 79 CE, burying these towns in several feet of volcanic ash and stone. When excavations began in the 1700s, archaeologists found these Roman cities almost perfectly preserved.

The Roman Empire declined after internal instability and attacks by Germanic tribes in the north. This period of unrest, which came to be called the Middle or Dark Ages, culminated with the Black Death in 1348. In Italy alone, about one third of the population died from this pandemic. Recovery from this calamity led to a resurgence or "Renaissance" of cities, trade, and economy, and as a result there was a boom in the arts, philosophy,

and science. You may have heard of the famous artists Leonardo Da Vinci, Michelangelo, and Botticelli, or of Galileo, the father of modern physics. They, and many more artists, architects, and thinkers, were all part of this rebirth. Their contributions influenced European art, science, and thought for centuries.

A period of foreign invasions and domination followed during the seventeenth to nineteenth centuries. These again led to a phase of social revolution. Finally, Italy was unified, or brought together, in 1861.

All of this history is very visible. It is said that 60 percent of the world's archaeological heritage is located in Italy. In fact, it is difficult to build new constructions in the cities. When workers start digging new foundations, more artifacts are found. Artists from all over the world have visited Italy to

Bay of Naples, with Mount Vesuvius in the background

find inspiration in all of this: from Gustave Flaubert and Goethe to Mark Twain and Henry James. Also, there are more UNESCO World Heritage sites in Italy than in any other country.

But Italy is not all about the past. It is the place where famous modern designers make everything from plates and pans (Alessi) to fashion (Prada and Giorgio Armani) and cars and motorbikes (Ferrari and Ducati). It is a place where millions of tourists enjoy breathtaking scenery, romantic sidewalk cafés, and, most of all, the great hospitality of the Italians.

ITALIAN CRAFTS
Cool Secrets for Creating Great Crafts

- Read through the instructions—all the way—before you start. This tip can be hard to follow, because you might be so eager to start, you'll dive right in. That's the right spirit! But read all the way through anyway. You'll be glad you did.
- Gather all your materials first. A missing item might make you stop halfway through, and then you won't feel like finishing.
- Protect your work surface. Lay down newspaper or a plastic tablecloth. Wear old clothes.
- Be creative. You might think of a great new step to add or a twist that gives the craft your personal touch. While you're at it, learn from your mistakes. Try a craft a few times to get it right. Your craft doesn't have to look like the one in the picture to be great.
- Be careful. When the instructions tell you to get help from an adult, *please get help from an adult!*
- Clean up right away. It's much easier to clean paintbrushes, wipe down surfaces, and wash tools (including your hands) while the mess is fresh.
- As you go about your everyday activities, save things that might be good for your projects. Shoeboxes, toilet paper rolls, ribbon and tissue paper from a gift—these can all be used to make crafts that you'll enjoy keeping or giving to friends and family.
- The final secret? Have fun! If you don't enjoy it, there's no point in crafting.

Grand Canal in Venice

La Bocca della Verità

La Bocca della Verità (The Mouth of Truth) is a large marble carving of a man-like face with a huge lion's mane, located in the entrance to a church in Italy's capital, Rome. The sculpture is thought to be part of a first-century fountain, portraying a pagan god.

Legend has it that the mouth functions as a lie detector: Starting from the Middle Ages, it was believed that if one told a lie with one's hand in the mouth of the sculpture, it would be bitten off. A famous Hollywood movie from the 1950s, *Roman Holiday,* shows a scene with *La Bocca della Verità.*

You can create the sculpture using plaster of paris and check if your friends are really telling the truth!

You'll Need:

Bocca della Verità: BOH-kah deh-lah VAYR-ee-tah

Old newspapers
Rubber gloves
Bucket
Plaster of paris
Large round aluminum pie pan or similar container
Nails, small spatula, or palette knife
Black paint
Paintbrush
Damp cloth or sandpaper

1. Cover your work surface with old newspapers.
2. Wearing gloves, mix the plaster of paris according to the package directions and pour it into the pan. Flatten it out with your palm. Then mold the eyes, nose, and mouth. Let it set until quite dry and firm.
3. Use a nail or other sharp object to scratch the beard, hair, and other features into the dried plaster of paris.
4. Lightly brush paint over the etched surface and wait until it dries.
5. Using a damp cloth or sandpaper, remove the surface paint until only the colored etching is left.

La Bocca della Verità

6. Once your sculpture is hard, turn it out onto your worktop. Prop it up on a shelf or mantelpiece for everyone to see and dare them to test *la bocca!*

The Leaning Tower of Pisa

The Leaning Tower of Pisa is one of Italy's most famous landmarks. It is the freestanding bell tower of the Campo dei Miracoli or Piazza dei Miracoli, which means "Field of Miracles." Located in the northern Italian city of Pisa, construction began in 1173—but the tower wasn't finished until 177 years later.

The tower began to lean in the early years of construction—the ground was simply softer on one side than the other. Several attempts have been made to right the tower, but some of them made the tower lean more.

After a soil scientist successfully steered the tower up in 1999, the tower leaned at an angle of about 4 degrees. The height of the tower is just over 183 feet (55.8 meters) from the ground on the low side and 186 feet (56.7 meters) on the high side. This puts the top of the tower 12 feet 10 inches (3.9 meters) over from where it would be if the structure were perfectly vertical.

You'll Need:

Large cardboard tube such as from stackable potato chips
Smaller cardboard tube such as a toilet paper roll
Cardboard support such as shoebox lid
White paper large enough to cover the large tube
Black, red, and green felt-tip pens
Glue
Clear tape
Scissors
Toothpick

1. Draw the arches of the main tower onto the paper with a black pen and glue the paper around the large tube. Do the same for the top part of the tower with the smaller and shorter tube.
2. Draw the Italian flag (vertical stripes of green, white, and red) and glue or tape it to the toothpick.

3. Glue the smaller tube on top of the large tube. Attach the toothpick flag at the top.
4. Trace the bottom of the larger tube onto the cardboard support. Cut halfway around the circle.
5. Insert the tower into the slot at an angle. You may have to use extra glue or tape to hold the tube in place.

Pisa: PEE-zah
Piazza dei Miracoli: PEE-ot-zah day MEER-uh-koh-lee

Murano Glass

During the Middle Ages, Venice became an important sea power and rich merchant city, trading goods such as silk and spices from the Byzantine Empire in Western Europe. As more people moved to Venice, the risk of fires increased. In 1291, because they used furnaces with high-temperature flames, all the glassmakers in Venice were forced to move to Murano, an island belonging to the city. In the following century the island became famous for glass products such as beads and mirrors. For a while Murano was the main producer of glass in Europe. It also became known for its chandeliers. Glassmaking is still the island's main industry.

You can use polymer clay to create the designs of Murano's millefiori ("thousand flowers") glass. Use your "glass" to make any object you like, such as beads, a pendant, a paperweight, or any kind of ornament.

You'll Need:

Polymer clay in different colors
Sharp knife
An adult
Needle or toothpick
Baking sheet
Oven
Oven mitts
Thread for pendants or bracelets

millefiori: mih-lih-fee-OR-ee

1. To create a flower effect, make lots of very thin sausages and flat squares with different colors of clay. The thinner you can make the sausages and the sheets, the finer your work will be.

Murano glassmakers also produce intricate animal designs.

2. Wrap a sheet around a sausage, or bundle more than 4 or 5 sausages with a different colored sheet. Gently roll the resulting, bigger sausage a little bit more. Repeat building and wrapping until the diameter of the resulting sausage is the size of the item you want to make.
3. With the help of **an adult,** slice the sausage with a very sharp knife. On the cut you will see beautiful patterns such as those of Murano glass jewelry.
4. Make holes with a needle or toothpick for beads or pendants. Place the pieces on a baking sheet and bake in the oven according to the manufacturer's instructions.

Ragdoll with Traditional Italian Costume

The title for this craft is actually a misnomer because there is no single traditional Italian costume. What is Italy today used to be several kingdoms. The unification, or Risorgimento, was a long process starting with the Congress of Vienna in 1815. It ended, more or less, in 1861 with the assembly of the first Italian parliament and the proclamation of Vittorio Emanuele II as King of Italy.

What follows is an approximation of a dress from Sardinia, Italy's second largest island. One can sometimes still see women wearing this traditional costume at *sagre,* or local festivals.

You'll Need:

Risorgimento: REE-sor-jee-men-toh

Craft paper
White or light cotton fabric (about 8 by 11 inches)
White thread and needle
Batting
Fabric marker
Yarn (whatever color you want for your doll's hair)
Old handkerchief or piece of lace
Red fabric for the skirt and small apron
Rubber band
Ribbon, costume necklace, decorative pins (optional)

1. Fold a piece of craft paper in half and draw the left half of the doll onto it, starting at the fold. It should look something like half a gingerbread man. Add ½ inch around the doll's outline for a seam allowance, and with **an adult's** help, cut along this outer line.

2. Unfold the paper and cut out 2 layers of white cotton fabric in the shape of this outline. Pin the pieces together, with right sides facing each other.

3. Sew them, leaving a little hole along the trunk of the doll. Reverse the fabric (turn the doll right side out). Stuff the doll with batting and sew the hole shut.

4. Draw a face with fabric marker, and glue or sew some yarn on its head for hair. Be sure to cover the back of its head as well. To make a headscarf, use a handkerchief or a piece of lace and lay it loosely over the doll's head.

5. Make a simple skirt by cutting a square the length of the doll's legs. Sew two sides together to create a tube, and drape the skirt around the doll's body. Use a rubber band like a belt to hold it in place.

6. To make the blouse, cut out a rectangle of white fabric, lay it over the doll's shoulders, and pin it together between the body and arms. Cut along the body up to the armpits (see photo). Cut the sleeves to make them straight. Sew together the back and front along the body and up the sleeve with a straight stitch and turn the blouse right side out. Put it on the doll and tuck it under the belt.

7. Make a large white or lacy apron by cutting a rectangle and tucking it under the belt. Make a smaller apron with red fabric and drape this over the larger apron.

8. You can decorate your doll further by attaching some ribbon to the bottom of the skirt or around its waist, and adding some gold chains or pins to the blouse.

Marbled Paper

Florence, a city in the Tuscany region in the north of Italy, was founded in Roman times, became very important during the Middle Ages, and sparked the Renaissance. Arts and crafts flourished during this "re-birth," and artisans in Florence have for centuries produced some of the world's finest diaries, journals, albums, and similar paper goods. Many of them are covered in or are decorated with marbled paper.

Although marbled paper probably originated in China, the Turks are most famous for developing this art, which they called *ebru*. Ebru arrived in Europe through Venice, which traded goods from Asia. Nowadays, Florence is famous for producing marbled paper.

You can use this marbled paper to make gift cards, maybe with matching wrapping paper; or you can glue it onto other objects as decoration.

You'll Need:

Lots of old newspaper
10 cups cold water
Shallow aluminum baking pan
Oil paints in matching colors
Turpentine
An adult
Gloves
Small jam jar with lid
Toothpick, old comb, plastic fork, or other disposable utensil
Brown wrapping paper, paper bags, or copier paper, smaller than the
    baking pan
Scissors
Stack of books (optional)

WARNING: Turpentine is flammable and toxic. Please work with an adult for this project.

1. Spread out several layers of newspaper to absorb any spills.
2. Place water in a shallow pan, then put on gloves.
3. Under **adult** supervision, mix the oil paints with a bit of turpentine. Start with a teaspoon of paint and a teaspoon of turpentine in a small jam jar, close it with a lid, and shake. Add turpentine or paint as needed until the paint is the consistency of thick cream.
4. Drop a few drops of color into the pan of water. If the color sinks, it is too thick, and you need to thin it with a little more turpentine. If the color spreads, it is too thin; add a little more paint. When the right thickness is achieved, drop large spots of color one at a time onto the water.
5. With a toothpick, comb, plastic fork, or other disposable utensil, very slowly and carefully swirl the paint into patterns. Make sure not to overmix because the result will be a gray blob.
6. Cut a piece of paper slightly smaller than the size of the pan. Holding opposite corners of the paper, gently lower it on to the solution. The design should stick to your paper.
7. Lift the paper carefully and place it right side up on newspapers to dry.
8. Let the paper dry for 24 hours. When it is completely dry, you can flatten it under a stack of books.

Mosaics

Mosaic is the art of assembling and attaching tiny colored glass or stone tiles to make a picture. The oldest mosaics we know are about 5,000 years old. Mosaics were very popular in Italy during Roman and medieval times. They covered everything from walls, floors, and ceilings to vases, plates, and other objects. A particularly beautiful example of mosaics is Villa Romana del Casale in Piazza Armerina in Sicily. Its 12,500 square feet (1,160 square meters) of mosaic flooring reflect the wealth and prestige of a senator or member of the Imperial family.

You can buy mosaic tiles in any craft shop, use small flat pebbles, or, with parental supervision, make your own tiles by gently smashing some old cups or plates inside a paper bag. Make a picture or cover an object such as a plate or picture frame.

You'll Need:

Mosaic tiles
Mosaic glue
Grout
Spatula
Rubber gloves
Rag
Vinegar

Villa Romana del Casale:
VEE-lah roh-MAH-nah del
kah-SAH-lee

1. Arrange the tiles on a support (for a picture) or your object to be covered (like a box lid). Glue them in place.
2. Mix the grout with water as per instructions on the box.
3. Wearing rubber gloves, use a spatula to spread the grout all over and around the mosaic tiles. Scrape off any excess grout.
4. After about 20 minutes, use a rag soaked in water and vinegar to carefully wipe off the extra grout from the tiles.
5. Let the grout dry overnight.

Colored Pasta Crafts

Pasta is one of Italy's biggest export articles, and each Italian eats an average of over 60 pounds (27 kilograms) of pasta per year. However, in the 1950s, it was considered exotic, and people in many parts of the world did not know much about it. In 1957, the British Broadcasting Company made a spoof documentary about pasta growing on trees. People asked the TV station to tell them where to buy these Spaghetti-Trees!

Pasta can be fresh or dried, long or short, filled or plain. Usually it is made from wheat, but it can also contain buckwheat or mashed potatoes. It can be homemade or industrially made. There are literally hundreds of varieties of pasta—but certainly none grows on trees!

You'll Need:

Different pasta shapes
Sealable plastic bags
Liquid food coloring
Vinegar
Measuring cup
Waxed paper
Glue
Cardboard support
String

1. Mix several drops of food coloring with ¼ cup of vinegar and ½ pound of pasta in a sealable plastic bag. Shake the pasta in the bag to spread the color evenly. Lay the pasta on waxed paper to dry completely.
2. Make a freestanding sculpture or glue the colored pasta to a sheet of cardboard for support. How about making a Ferrari, a gladiator, or a colorful bowl of gelato?
3. Thread the pasta pieces onto string to make a necklace or bracelet.

Venetian Carnival Mask

The Carnival of Venice is probably the most famous festival of Italy. As the name suggests, it is held every year in Venice two weeks before Ash Wednesday, a solemn day that signifies the beginning of Lent. Carnival ends on Fat Tuesday or Mardi Gras, the day before Ash Wednesday. Masks have been an important part of Carnival and have special names according to their shape: Moretta (made of black velvet), Bauta (which covers all or most of the face), the Volto or Larva (a white mask that originally covered only part of the face to allow the wearer to eat and drink), and the Dottore Peste (which has a beak and was worn by plague doctors, who believed that herbs in the beak would protect them from infection). Mask makers have been so important to Venice that they were allowed to form their own guild in the fifteenth century, and it is still thriving.

You'll Need:

Blank mask from a craft store
Gold paint
Feathers
Glue
Ribbon
Pearls, glitter, and other decorations

> Dottore Peste: DOH-tor-ay PES-teh

1. On the mask, paint the area around the eyes gold.
2. Glue feathers around the outer edge. Glue a strip of ribbon over the feathers' ends.
3. You can add some pearls or glitter around the eyes as well.
4. Wear your mask with a long dark veil or cloak to the next costume party!

Nativity

At Christmastime all across Italy, and especially in Rome, Nativity scenes are displayed in most homes, churches, and "piazzas" or town squares. Also called crèches, these dioramas show the baby Jesus lying in the manger, with his parents Mary and Joseph, the shepherds, and various animals looking on.

According to tradition, the youngest member of the house places the baby Jesus into the manger on Christmas Eve. The Three Kings are not placed in the crèche until January 6, the day of the Epiphany. Figures are made from all kinds of materials, from papier mâché to wood or plastic, with elaborate stables and sceneries. There are famous centers of crèche production in Naples, Lecce, and other Italian cities. You can make the figures from salt dough and arrange them in a decorated shoebox.

You'll Need:

1 cup table salt
1 cup white flour
Water
Toothpicks or small palette knife
Oven or microwave
An adult
Shoebox or other small carton
Paint (optional)
Straw and sticks, brown paper (optional)

1. Mix salt and flour in a large bowl. Add just enough water to make a firm dough, and knead thoroughly. Make different-sized balls for heads, torsos, and legs. Stick them together and shape them so that they can stand up. Don't forget to make the manger.

2. Use toothpicks or the palette knife to add eyes, hair, clothing folds, and other details. If you want, you can paint the faces and clothes after the figures have dried.
3. With the help of **an adult,** dry the dough in the oven at 300°F or for a few minutes in the microwave.
4. Decorate a shoebox with some straw and sticks, brown paper, and whatever else you'd like to put in the scene. Arrange the figures in the shoebox, and place the crèche on a mantel or table.

Befana—The Witch's Stocking

In popular folklore, the Befana is an old witch who rides on a broomstick. She visits all the children of Italy on the eve of Epiphany (the night of January 5) and fills their stockings with candy and presents if they have been good or a lump of coal or dark candy if they have misbehaved. Being a good housekeeper, she will sweep the floor before she leaves. The child's family typically leaves a small glass of wine and a plate with a few morsels of food for the Befana.

You'll Need:

Befana: BAY-fah-nah

2 pieces of felt or other thick fabric
Thread and needle
Ribbon in matching color, 4 inches long
Felt pieces in different colors
Scissors
Glue
Fabric pen to draw face

1. Cut out 2 pieces of felt in a stocking shape, about 6 inches by 12 inches. Hem the tops, then sew the pieces together, with right sides together, leaving the top open.
2. Using a piece of ribbon, make a loop for hanging the stocking. Sew the loop inside the stocking at the top in the back. Turn the stocking right side out.
3. From the felt, cut out the parts of the Befana: her hat, face, upper body, arms and hands, skirt, feet, and broom. Add extra patches to her coat if you want. Glue the pieces to the stocking.
4. Tell your parents about the Befana, so they can let her know if you've been good or bad!

Italian Food

Cooking and eating good food are central elements of Italian culture. It starts with picking out the very best produce, which is often done in the daily market or in specialty shops. Preparation often involves a lot of time and several people.

Eating together is important, and Sunday lunches often go on for hours. No wonder. Everybody wants to show his or her appreciation for the cook, and it takes a lot of time to eat the many small courses that make up a traditional meal: *antipasti* (starters, such as salami or other cold cuts, marinated vegetables, or olives), *primo piatto* (usually a pasta or risotto dish), *secondo piatto* (meat or, as is often the case on the eve of an important holiday, fish), *contorno* (side dish of vegetables), *frutta* (fruit), *dolce* (dessert), and *caffè* (coffee).

Italian food is not all about pasta and pizza. The so-called Mediterranean diet, with lots of fruit, vegetables, pulses, and high-quality—usually extra virgin—olive oil is considered extremely healthy.

Olive oil is made by crushing olives and then extracting the oil from the pulp. It comes in various grades of quality, with extra virgin, cold-pressed olive oil being the highest grade. Olives are grown all across Italy, with the most production in the south and center. When you buy olive oil, check that it is not mixed with other oils or extracted by chemical means.

Some of the recipes in this book call for tomato puree, which is made of tomatoes that have been cooked briefly and strained. It is thicker than tomato sauce, which is often seasoned. If you can't find tomato puree in your store, you can use crushed tomatoes.

Buon appetito!

Tips for the Kitchen

- Read through the recipe—*all the way*—before you start.
- Wear an apron to protect your clothes.
- Wash your hands with warm water and soap before you start and after handling raw meat.
- Be careful! Always get help from **an adult** when you are using the oven, the stovetop, or sharp knives. Use oven mitts to lift hot lids, baking sheets, and pans. Protect the counter with a trivet before you set down a hot container.
- Clean up right away.
- Finally, share your food with your friends and family. Seeing people enjoy your cooking is as much fun as enjoying it yourself!

Minestrone—Vegetable Soup

Minestrone means "big soup." It can contain all kinds of vegetables, beans, and either rice or pasta in small shapes. The ingredients vary by region and, most of all, by season. It is usually served with a drop of high quality olive oil and Parmesan cheese (*Parmigiano*) sprinkled over the top. For an authentic minestrone, find vegetables that are fresh—maybe in a farmer's market—and that you like, or follow the list of ingredients here and prepare the winter version below.

Preparation Time: 20 minutes
Cooking Time: 30 minutes
Servings: 6

Ingredients:

4	celery ribs
½	cabbage, any kind
2	leeks, white part only
2	medium carrots
1	bunch Swiss chard
3	quarts hot water
1	bay leaf (fresh, if you can find it)
½	bunch of flat-leaf parsley (also called Italian parsley)
20	whole peppercorns
	Salt
1	piece Parmigiano-Reggiano rind (optional)
10	cherry tomatoes
	Small shape (egg) Pasta
	Freshly grated Parmigiano
	Extra virgin olive oil

> I like to boil the pasta separately and add it directly to the bowl. If you boil the pasta in the big soup pot and you don't eat all the soup, you will have very soggy pasta for leftovers.

1. Wash, peel, and chop all the vegetables into bite-sized pieces.
2. Put all of them except the tomatoes in a large pot with the hot water. Add the spices and about a level tablespoon of salt. Bring to a boil, then turn down the heat to medium low.
3. In a separate pan, cook the pasta according to package directions. When the pasta is done, drain it and set it aside.
4. After 20 minutes, check the vegetables for doneness. If they are ready, add the tomatoes and Parmigiano-Reggiano rind and cook for a few more minutes.
5. Place half a cup or so of pasta into each serving bowl. Spoon the soup over the pasta, then drizzle some olive oil and sprinkle grated cheese over it.

minestrone: mih-nih-STROH-nee

Bucatini All'Amatriciana—Spicy Pasta

Pasta is usually served as a *primo piatto* (first dish) and can appear in soup (such as tortellini), baked in the oven (lasagna), filled (agnolotti or ravioli), or plain. It may be short or long (bucatini is long and straight with a hole running through the center) and served with any of dozens of sauces. There are huge regional variations in the way pasta is served as well. This recipe is from Italy's capital, Rome.

Guanciale is lean, unsmoked bacon, taken from pig jowls, and it has a rich pork flavor. You can substitute regular bacon or pancetta (seasoned Italian bacon), but the dish won't be as flavorful.

Preparation Time: 10 minutes
Cooking Time: 35 minutes
Servings: 4

Ingredients:

2	tablespoons extra virgin olive oil
1	garlic clove, peeled
¼	teaspoon dried crushed red pepper (to taste)
4	ounces guanciale, cut into small cubes
1	pound tomatoes, chopped (about 3 cups)
12	ounces bucatini or spaghetti
¾	cup freshly grated Pecorino Romano or Parmesan cheese

Pecorino Romano is a hard, salty cheese made from sheep's milk.

1. With **adult** help, heat the oil in a skillet over medium-low. Add garlic and red pepper; sauté about 2 minutes.
2. Add the guanciale and fry about 10 minutes.

3. Stir in the tomatoes; simmer until the tomatoes disintegrate—about 20 minutes.
4. Season sauce with salt and freshly ground black pepper.
5. Meanwhile, cook the pasta in a large pot of boiling salted water until still quite firm. Return the pasta to the pot and add the sauce. Toss them together, cooking the mixture gently for a minute or two more until the pasta is al dente.
6. Sprinkle with the grated cheese and serve.

agnolotti: on-yuh-LAH-tee
guanciale: gwahn-TCHAH-leh
pancetta: pan-CHEH-tuh

Frittata—Egg Dish

Frittata is a very versatile and nutritious egg dish similar to the French omelet. You can add any type of ingredients, from ham and cheeses to vegetables, mushrooms, and fresh herbs. Leftover pasta or rice can also be added to a frittata. As with most other Italian food, one may find great regional and seasonal differences in this dish: wild mushrooms in the mountains, fish or seafood by the sea; zucchini in the summer and artichokes in the winter.

Preparation Time: 10 minutes
Cooking Time: 10 minutes
Servings: 2

frittata: frih-TAH-tah

Ingredients:

2	tablespoons extra virgin olive oil
4	eggs
1	cup ham, cheese, leftover pasta or rice, or fresh herbs
	Salt
	Pepper

> To flip the frittata, slide it out of the pan and onto a plate that is larger than the pan, then cover the frittata with the pan turned upside down. Flip the plate and pan around together so that the pan is again right side up with the frittata in it.

1. Chop your chosen filling into small pieces. You can have as many different items as you want, but they should add up to 1 cup all together.
2. Beat the eggs in a bowl, then add a good pinch of salt and pepper along with the filling.

3. With **adult** help, heat the oil till medium hot in a small frying pan. Add the egg mixture and let it cook gently without stirring until it is firm around the edges.
4. Using a large plate, flip the frittata over and cook for another couple of minutes, until the egg is no longer runny.
5. Serve with a green salad on the side or pack it for a nutritious boxed lunch.

Lenticchie—
Lentil Stew

A dish that is on almost every Italian table on New Year's Eve are lentils. They are considered auspicious—bringing good luck and fortune. I always thought that they represented coins and eating them would make me rich. The funny thing with lentil stew is that it is served at midnight when everybody has already had a huge array of *antipasti, primo piatto, secondo piatto,* and so on. Some dinner guests eat only a token spoonful because everybody is already stuffed, which is a shame because it is yummy!

New Year's Eve lentils are often cooked with *cotechino* (a fatty pork sausage) or *zampone* (pig's trotter filled with fatty pork sausage). Since you may have difficulty finding these specialty items and they are quite an acquired taste, I present you with a simpler version.

Preparation Time: 10 minutes plus overnight soaking
Cooking Time: 1 hour 10 minutes
Servings: 6

Ingredients:

1¼ cups dried lentils
1 small onion
3 ounces bacon or pancetta
1 14-ounce can tomato puree
3 tablespoons extra virgin olive oil
1 cup beef stock
 Salt and pepper

> lenticchie: len-TEEK-yay
> cotechino: koh-tay-KEE-noh
> zampone: ZAM-poh-nay

1. Let the lentils soak in a large bowl of cold water overnight.
2. With **an adult's** help, gently sauté the onion and the pancetta over low heat in the oil until the onion is soft.
3. Add the lentils, tomato puree, and about a cup of stock. Cook on low heat for one hour, stirring occasionally. You may have to add a little more broth so that the lentils don't dry out too much. Season with salt and pepper.

Pizza Margherita

Margherita: mar-GAYR-ee-tah

Everybody knows pizza! The original version comes from Naples and is made with a soft yeast dough baked in a special wood-fired pizza oven. Many people also like Roman-style pizza, which has a much thinner and crunchier crust. Some pizza purists say that only Pizza Marinara (with a garlicky tomato sauce) and Pizza Margherita are the real thing, but, of course, everybody has his or her own favorite topping. Some eat only white pizza—that is, without tomato sauce—but for others it is not pizza if it doesn't have tomato sauce and mozzarella cheese on it. Here is the simplest form of the pizza—just add any toppings you like.

Preparation Time: 3½ hours
Cooking Time: 20 minutes
Servings: 4

Ingredients:

¾   cup warm water (105°–115°F)
1½ teaspoons active dry yeast
2   cups unbleached all-purpose flour
1   teaspoon salt

¾   cup tomato puree
2   tablespoons extra virgin olive oil
6   ounces fresh mozzarella, cut into ¼-inch-thick slices
    Oregano
    Any other toppings you'd like, such as fresh tomatoes or mushrooms, sliced bell peppers or zucchini, or meats such as pepperoni, sausage, or bacon. If you use sausage or bacon, be sure it is thoroughly cooked before you put it on the pizza.

1. Stir together yeast, 1 tablespoon flour, and ¼ cup warm water in a large bowl and let it stand until the surface appears creamy, about 5 minutes.

2. Sift the rest of the flour and the salt into the yeast mixture and add the remaining water. Knead the dough for about 10 minutes, by which time it should be elastic.
3. Put the doughball in a clean bowl and cover the bowl with a tea towel. Leave it in a warm place for about 3 hours.
4. Preheat the oven to 475°F. Roll out the dough to about ½ inch thick on an oiled baking sheet. Spread a little bit of tomato puree on the dough, then drizzle some olive oil on it. Bake for about 15 minutes.
5. Using oven mitts, remove the pizza from the oven. Add the mozzarella and oregano and any other toppings you like. Bake for an extra 5 minutes. Let the pizza cool for a few minutes before slicing it.

Saltimbocca Alla Romana— Roman Veal Cutlets

Saltimbocca means this dish "jumps into the mouth." It is a very tasty and easy-to-prepare meat dish. Most people associate it with Rome but it is cooked all across Italy, sometimes with a slice of cheese added. The original recipe is made with a white wine sauce. The alcohol in the recipe dissipates during cooking, but if cooking with wine is not permitted in your home, you can substitute it with the same amount of chicken broth. Eat it with a side dish of sautéed or steamed vegetables and some crusty Italian bread.

Preparation Time: 15 minutes
Cooking Time: 10 minutes
Servings: 4

saltimbocca alla romana: sal-teem-BOH-kah ah-lah roh-MAH-nah
prosciutto: PROH-shoo-toh

Ingredients:

8   thin veal cutlets (less than
     $\frac{1}{8}$ inch thick, about 2½ ounces each)
     salt and pepper
8   fresh large sage leaves (each about 2½ to 3 inches long)
8   thin slices prosciutto
3   tablespoons extra virgin olive oil
²⁄₃ cup dry white wine or chicken broth

1. If the cutlets are not thin enough, lay them on a cutting board and beat them with a meat mallet or a rolling pin to flatten them a bit.
2. On each piece of veal, lay first a piece of prosciutto and then a sage leaf. Thread them together with a wooden toothpick.
3. With **adult** help, heat half of the olive oil over medium high heat and add half of the meat in a single layer in the pan. Fry for 1 or 2 minutes on each side. Put the first batch of meat onto a plate.

4. Repeat step 3 with the second batch, adding more oil if needed.
5. Return all meat to the pan, add the wine or broth, and let it bubble
   up nicely for another minute or two.

Parmigiana di Melanzane— Eggplant Parmesan

We don't know exactly why the dish Parmigiana, meaning "from Parma," is called that. It is not a dish typical of or originating from Parma in northern Italy; it actually comes from the south, either Sicily or Campania. It is made with layers of fried eggplant, cheese, and tomato sauce. If you substitute zucchini for eggplant, the dish will be called *zucchine alla Parmigiana.*

Preparation Time: 45 minutes
Cooking Time: 50 minutes
Servings: 4

Ingredients:

Parmigiana di melanzane: par-mud-JAH-nah dee meh-lon-ZAH-nay
zucchine alla Parmigiana: dzoo-KEE-nay ah-lah par-mud-JAH-nah

3	firm eggplants
½	cup olive oil
1	small onion, finely sliced
20	ounces tomato puree
	a handful of basil leaves
½	pound mozzarella, sliced (or use shredded mozzarella)
6	tablespoons Parmesan cheese
	Salt
	Pepper
	Pinch of sugar

Tomatoes are naturally slightly acidic, the more so if they do not get a lot of sun before they are picked. Adding a pinch of sugar to the tomato sauce lowers its acidity.

1. Wash the eggplants. Remove the stems, and cut lengthwise into slices not thicker than ¼ inch.
2. Fill a large platter with a layer of slices, sprinkle them with salt, add another layer of eggplant, salt, etc. until you have used up all eggplant. Place a weight on top (you can use a large pot filled with water), and let stand for about one hour.
3. In the meantime, sweat the onion in oil over very low heat. They should not get brown. Then add the tomato puree and let simmer for about half an hour, stirring frequently. Toward the end, add the fresh basil leaves and adjust the seasoning with a pinch of sugar or salt if necessary.
4. Cut the mozzarella into very thin slices and let them dry on a cloth.
5. Wash the salt off the eggplant and dry the pieces with a paper towel. Fry them in batches in some olive oil so that they are nicely browned on both sides.
6. Preheat the oven to 375°F. Spread a little tomato sauce in a deep baking dish and cover it with a layer of eggplant. Sprinkle with Parmesan cheese, pour on a layer of tomato sauce, and cover with slices of mozzarella. Repeat this layering until all the ingredients have been used, ending with tomato sauce. Sprinkle with more grated Parmesan cheese and bake for about 30 minutes or until it has a nice brown crust.
7. Let it cool before serving—you can even eat it at room temperature.

Crostata Alle Ciliegie— Cherry Pie

This is our Nonna (Grandma) Graziella's recipe for a *crostata,* which is the Italian version of sweet pie. Traditionally pies are made with a filling of jam, such as apricot, peach, or cherry; or with a custard-like *crema pasticcera* (pastry cream) or a sweet ricotta (cheese) filling. Italians eat this treat for breakfast. Imagine starting the day with a fragrant *crostata alle ciliegie!*

Preparation Time: 50 minutes
including resting time
Cooking Time: 40 minutes
Servings: 12

Crostata Alle Ciliegie:
KROH-stah-tah AL-eh CHEE-lee-ay-jeh
crema pasticcera : KRAY-mah pah-stee-CHAY-rah
nonna: NOH-nah

Ingredients:

2½   cups all-purpose flour
      a pinch of salt
½   cup sugar
      finely grated fresh lemon zest from 1 lemon
1   large egg plus 2 egg yolks, lightly beaten
1½   sticks (¾ cup) unsalted butter, softened
2   cups cherry jam

> To zest a lemon, wash and dry the fruit, then grate off just the brightly colored outer rind. Wrap up the rest of the lemon and refrigerate to save for another recipe.

1. On a clean worktop, mix the flour with the salt, sugar, and lemon zest.
2. Make a well and add the eggs and the softened butter in pieces. Knead only long enough to mix the ingredients thoroughly.
3. Roll out ⅔ of the pastry between two sheets of plastic wrap or waxed paper. Lay it in a buttered pie pan. Cover it with a tea towel and let it rest in a cool place for half an hour.
4. Preheat the oven to 350°F.

5. Spread the jam over the pastry. Make strips of the remaining dough and lay them over the jam in a crisscross pattern.
6. Bake for about 35-40 minutes or until the crust has a nice golden color.

Chiacchiere—Fried Carnival Pastry

Carnival pastry exists all across Italy and has many different names: *chiacchiere* ("gossips") or *lattughe* ("lettuces") in Lombardia, *cenci* and *donzelle* in Toscana, *frappe* and *sfrappole* in Emilia, *bugie* ("lies") in Piemonte, and so on. It is usually fried dough sprinkled with confectioner's sugar, honey, raisins, and pine nuts or sometimes colorful sugar sprinkles. In ancient times the pastry was fried in lard; nowadays oil is more usual. It probably comes from the Roman sweet *frictilia,* which was prepared in big quantities during Carnival so that it could then be eaten during the fasting period leading up to Easter.

Preparation Time: 30 minutes plus 1 hour resting time
Cooking Time: 30 minutes
Servings: 4

Ingredients:

3½ cups all-purpose flour
1   pinch salt
2   tablespoons confectioner's sugar
3   eggs
1   tablespoon milk
1   teaspoon vanilla extract
     Vegetable oil for frying
     Confectioner's sugar

1. Mix the flour, sugar, and salt on a pastry board, then make a well. Break the eggs into the center and add the milk and the vanilla.
2. Knead for about 10 minutes, moistening the dough with an additional spoonful of milk, if needed.

3. Wrap the dough in a cloth and let it rest in a cool place for about one hour.
4. Knead it again for a short while and then roll it out to about ⅛ inch thick.
5. Cut the dough with a pastry wheel to make strips that are 3 inches wide and 4 inches long. Use the wheel to make three lengthwise slits on each piece.
6. With **adult** help, heat the frying oil in a deep pan. When the oil is hot, fry the pieces of dough.
7. Drain them on paper towels. Serve warm or cold, on a napkin-lined serving dish, generously sprinkled with confectioner's sugar.

chiacchiere: kee-AH-kyay-ray
lattughe: lah-TOO-gay
cenci: CHEEN-chee
donzelle: don-ZAY-lay
sfrappole: s-FRAH-poh-lay
bugie: boo-JEE-eh

Frollini— Cookies

In Italy, cookies are often dipped into morning milk or coffee. These versatile *frollini* are made with a simple, unleavened dough similar to that used for *crostata*. You can make them in any shape you like, so they can be used for decorating the tree at Christmas or the festive table at Easter.

Preparation Time: 1 hour including resting time
Cooking Time: 20 minutes
Servings: 4

Ingredients:

7 tablespoons butter at room temperature
½ cup confectioner's sugar
1 egg yolk
½ teaspoon vanilla extract
1¼ cups flour
2 tablespoons cornstarch
 Icing, sugar pearls (optional)

frollini: FROH-lee-nee

1. Mix the butter, sugar, egg yolk, and vanilla until light and creamy.
2. Sift in the flour, cornstarch, and a pinch of salt. Knead well to make a firm dough, wrap it in plastic wrap, and let it rest in the fridge for 30 minutes.
3. Preheat the oven to 325°F.
4. Roll out the dough between two sheets of plastic wrap or waxed paper to between ⅛ and ¼ inch thick.

5. Cut out shapes with cookie cutters of your choice. If you want to hang them on your Christmas tree, make a hole with a toothpick at the top of each cookie.
6. Place the cookies on a greased baking sheet. Bake them for 18 minutes or until they are golden brown.
7. Let them cool on the baking sheet for a minute or two, then transfer them to a cooling rack.
8. When they are completely cool, decorate them with icing and sugar pearls or other edible decorations.

Further Reading

Books

Blashfield, Jean F. *Italy*. Danbury, Conn.: Children's Press, 2008.

Collodi, Carlo. *The Adventures of Pinocchio (Le Avventure Di Pinocchio): The Complete Text in a Bilingual Edition with the Original Illustrations.* Translated by Nicolas J. Perella. Berkeley and Los Angeles: University of California Press, 2005.

Deem, James M. *Bodies From the Ash: Life and Death in Ancient Pompeii.* New York: Houghton Mifflin Books for Children, 2005.

DiPrimio, Pete. *How'd They Do That in Ancient Rome?* Hockessin, Del.: Mitchell Lane Publishers, 2009.

Editors of Phaidon Press. *The Silver Spoon for Children: Favorite Italian Recipes.* London, England: Phaidon Press, 2009.

Green, Jen. *Focus on Italy.* New York: World Almanac Library, 2007.

Mann, Elizabeth. *The Roman Colosseum: The Story of the World's Most Famous Stadium and Its Deadly Games.* New York: Mikaya Press, 2006.

Works Consulted

This book is based on the author's experiences living in Italy, on family recipes, and on the following sources:

Bay, Alan. *La cucina italiana: Ricette d'oro.* Milan, Italy: Piemme, 2009.

BBC: On This Day. "1957: BBC Fools the Nation." http://news.bbc.co.uk/onthisday/hi/dates/stories/april/1/newsid_2819000/2819261.stm

Craft Ideas: Mosaic Tutorial http://www.craftideas.info/html/mosaic_tutorial_b.html

Editors of Phaidon Press. *The Silver Spoon.* London, England: Phaidon Press, 2005.

Epicurious http://www.epicurious.com/

La Cucina Italiana http://lacucinaitalianamagazine.com

UNESCO World Heritage Centre http://whc.unesco.org/en/list/

Zanini De Vita, Oretta. *Encyclopedia of Pasta.* Translated by Maureen B. Fant. Berkeley and Los Angeles: University of California Press, 2009.

Further Reading

On the Internet

Italian Craft Projects for Kids
http://www.ehow.com/way_5730777_italian-craft-projects-kids.html#ixzz19T2ix4la

Italian Trade Commission: Italian Made
http://www.ItalianMade.com

NOVA Online: "Fall of the Leaning Tower"
http://www.pbs.org/wgbh/nova/pisa/interventions.html

Glossary

al dente (al DEN-tay)—Cooked just enough to be still firm but not hard.

Carnival (KAR-nee-vahl)— A big outdoor celebration just before Lent, including parades and costumes.

diet (DY-et)—The sum of food a person eats.

dissipate (DIH-sih-payt)—To break up and scatter or vanish.

dolce vita (DOHL-chay VEE-tah)—Sweet life.

Epiphany (ee-PIH-fuh-nee)—A Christian holiday on January 6 celebrating the visit of the Magi (Three Kings, or Three Wise Men) to the infant Jesus.

gelato (jeh-LAH-toh)— Italian ice cream made with sugar, cream, and fruit, nuts, or other flavoring.

guild (GILD)—A powerful association of craftsmen in a particular trade in the Middle Ages.

Lent—A period of six weeks of fasting leading up to Easter.

Middle Ages—A period in European history that lasted roughly from the fifth to the fifteenth century. It was also called the Dark Ages.

mosaic (moh-ZAY-ik)—A piece of art made by assembling small pieces of glass or stone on a supporting surface to create an image.

Nativity (nuh-TIH-vih-tee)—The scene of the birth of Jesus.

pagan (PAY-gan)— Referring to pre-Christian religions that often included more than one god.

plague (PLAYG)—A deadly disease that spreads rapidly and infects many people. The Black Death of the Middle Ages has been identified as bubonic (boo-BAH-nik) plague, which was carried by fleas and rats. Millions of people died in Europe, Africa, and Asia during this plague.

Renaissance (REH-nuh-zahntz)—The rebirth of thought, art, and expression that occurred in Europe after the Middle Ages.

Roman Empire—A large area of Europe and the Mediterranean Sea ruled from Rome in the period from the first century BCE to the mid-fifteenth century CE.

sauté—To cook in a light layer of oil over medium heat, stirring constantly, until done but not brown.

spoof—A humorous trick or hoax.

sweat—To cook in a light layer of oil over very low heat with the lid on, stirring once in a while, until done but not brown.

unleavened (un-LEH-vund)—A dough product such as bread or batter having no rising ingredients.

Index

ABOUT THE
AUTHOR

Julia Harms was born in Hamburg, Germany, and now lives in Switzerland. Through her work with the United Nations, she began to travel the world. She has worked on and off in Italy since 1994, and lived in the lovely city of Turin in Italy's Piemonte region for three years. She married a wonderful man from Brindisi in the Apulia region in 2002. Together with her husband and their three daughters, she travels to Italy regularly to visit family and friends, sample the wonderful food, and discover new treasures of Italian culture.